# THE BLUEPRINT: PROJECT PLANNER

JENEVA M. STEVENS

**author**HOUSE®

*AuthorHouse™*
*1663 Liberty Drive*
*Bloomington, IN 47403*
*www.authorhouse.com*
*Phone: 833-262-8899*

*Published by AuthorHouse  12/14/2022*

*ISBN: 978-1-6655-7725-0 (sc)*
*ISBN: 978-1-6655-7723-6 (hc)*
*ISBN: 978-1-6655-7724-3 (e)*

This Book Belongs To:

Name: _____

Phone: _____

Email: _____

# TABLE OF CONTENTS

# THE BLUEPRINT: PROJECT PLANNER

May all your projects go without a hitch. -Jeneva S.

**Project 1:**

**Month:**_____ **Week Of:**_____ **Start Date:**_____ **Due Date:**_____

**Priority:**

**Schedule/ Reschedule:**

**Inquire/ Look Into:**

**Log:**

**Print:**

**Email/ Call:**

**Follow Up:**

**Pay/Submit:**

**Don't Forget:**

*The Blueprint: Project Planner*

**Workflow Objective:**

**Phase 1: Initiate:**

**Phase 2: Execute:**

**Phase 3: Monitor:**

**Phase 4: Approve:**

**Phase 5: Wrap Up:**

**Critical Details:**

**Stakeholders:**

**Important Milestones:**

**Quick Contacts:**

| No. | Task: | Purpose: | Completion Date: | Completed? Yes | No |
|-----|-------|----------|------------------|----------------|-----|
| 1 | | | | | |
| 2 | | | | | |
| 3 | | | | | |
| 4 | | | | | |
| 5 | | | | | |
| 6 | | | | | |
| 7 | | | | | |
| 8 | | | | | |
| 9 | | | | | |
| 10 | | | | | |
| 11 | | | | | |
| 12 | | | | | |
| 13 | | | | | |
| 14 | | | | | |
| 15 | | | | | |
| 16 | | | | | |
| 17 | | | | | |
| 18 | | | | | |
| 19 | | | | | |
| 20 | | | | | |
| 21 | | | | | |
| 22 | | | | | |
| 23 | | | | | |
| 24 | | | | | |

|  | Important | Not Important |
|---|---|---|
| Urgent | | |
| Non-Urgent | | |

| Important Dates: | Events/ Occasions: | Dress Attire: | Time: |
|---|---|---|---|
| | | | |
| | | | |
| | | | |
| | | | |
| | | | |
| | | | |
| | | | |
| | | | |
| | | | |
| | | | |
| | | | |
| | | | |
| | | | |

**Goals:**
1.
2.
3.

**Tomorrow's Focus:**
1.
2.
3.

**Work Motivation:**
1.
2.
3.

**Personal Motivation:**
1.
2.
3.

*The Blueprint: Project Planner*

_Lingering Thoughts:_

**Project 2:**

**Month:**_____ **Week Of:**_____ **Start Date:**_____ **Due Date:**_____

**Priority:**

**Schedule/ Reschedule:**

**Inquire/ Look Into:**

**Log:**

**Print:**

**Email/ Call:**

**Follow Up:**

**Pay/Submit:**

**Don't Forget:**

*The Blueprint: Project Planner*

**Workflow Objective:**

**Phase 1: Initiate:**

**Phase 2: Execute:**

**Phase 3: Monitor:**

**Phase 4: Approve:**

**Phase 5: Wrap Up:**

**Critical Details:**

**Stakeholders:**

**Important Milestones:**

**Quick Contacts:**

| No. | Task: | Purpose: | Completion Date: | Completed? Yes No |
|-----|-------|----------|------------------|------------------|
| 1 | | | | |
| 2 | | | | |
| 3 | | | | |
| 4 | | | | |
| 5 | | | | |
| 6 | | | | |
| 7 | | | | |
| 8 | | | | |
| 9 | | | | |
| 10 | | | | |
| 11 | | | | |
| 12 | | | | |
| 13 | | | | |
| 14 | | | | |
| 15 | | | | |
| 16 | | | | |
| 17 | | | | |
| 18 | | | | |
| 19 | | | | |
| 20 | | | | |
| 21 | | | | |
| 22 | | | | |
| 23 | | | | |
| 24 | | | | |

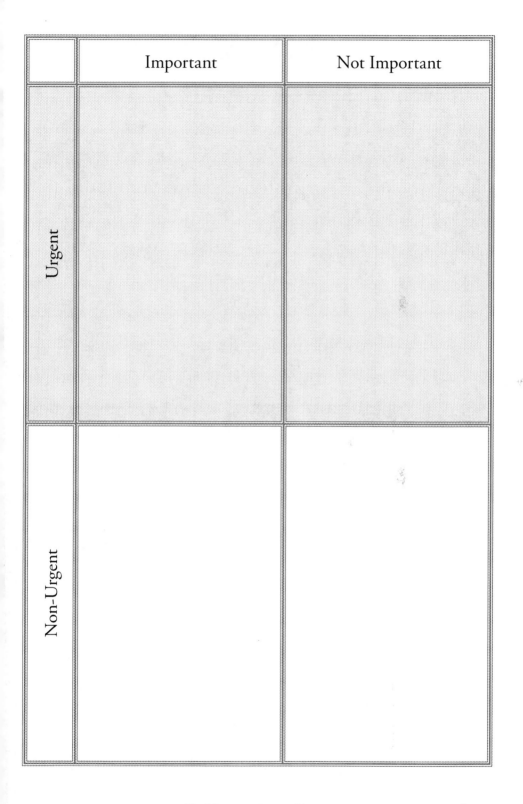

|  | Important | Not Important |
|---|---|---|
| **Urgent** |  |  |
| **Non-Urgent** |  |  |

| Important Dates: | Events/ Occasions: | Dress Attire: | Time: |
|---|---|---|---|
|  |  |  |  |
|  |  |  |  |
|  |  |  |  |
|  |  |  |  |
|  |  |  |  |
|  |  |  |  |
|  |  |  |  |
|  |  |  |  |
|  |  |  |  |
|  |  |  |  |
|  |  |  |  |
|  |  |  |  |
|  |  |  |  |
|  |  |  |  |

**Goals:**
1.
2.
3.

**Tomorrow's Focus:**
1.
2.
3.

**Work Motivation:**
1.
2.
3.

**Personal Motivation:**
1.
2.
3.

*Lingering Thoughts:*

**Project 3:**

**Month:**_____ **Week Of:**_____ **Start Date:**_____ **Due Date:**_____

**Priority:**

**Schedule/ Reschedule:**

**Inquire/ Look Into:**

**Log:**

**Print:**

**Email/ Call:**

**Follow Up:**

**Pay/Submit:**

**Don't Forget:**

**Workflow Objective:**

**Phase 1: Initiate:**

**Phase 2: Execute:**

**Phase 3: Monitor:**

**Phase 4: Approve:**

**Phase 5: Wrap Up:**

**Critical Details:**

**Stakeholders:**

**Important Milestones:**

**Quick Contacts:**

| No. | Task: | Purpose: | Completion Date: | Completed? | |
|-----|-------|----------|------------------|------------|---|
| | | | | Yes | No |
| 1 | | | | | |
| 2 | | | | | |
| 3 | | | | | |
| 4 | | | | | |
| 5 | | | | | |
| 6 | | | | | |
| 7 | | | | | |
| 8 | | | | | |
| 9 | | | | | |
| 10 | | | | | |
| 11 | | | | | |
| 12 | | | | | |
| 13 | | | | | |
| 14 | | | | | |
| 15 | | | | | |
| 16 | | | | | |
| 17 | | | | | |
| 18 | | | | | |
| 19 | | | | | |
| 20 | | | | | |
| 21 | | | | | |
| 22 | | | | | |
| 23 | | | | | |
| 24 | | | | | |

| | Important | Not Important |
|---|---|---|
| **Urgent** | | |
| **Non-Urgent** | | |

| Important Dates: | Events/ Occasions: | Dress Attire: | Time: |
|---|---|---|---|
| | | | |
| | | | |
| | | | |
| | | | |
| | | | |
| | | | |
| | | | |
| | | | |
| | | | |
| | | | |
| | | | |
| | | | |
| | | | |

## Goals:
1.
2.
3.

**Tomorrow's Focus:**
1.
2.
3.

**Work Motivation:**
1.
2.
3.

**Personal Motivation:**
1.
2.
3.

*Lingering Thoughts:*

**Project 4:**

**Month:**_____ **Week Of:**_____ **Start Date:**_____ **Due Date:**_____

**Priority:**

**Schedule/ Reschedule:**

**Inquire/ Look Into:**

**Log:**

**Print:**

**Email/ Call:**

**Follow Up:**

**Pay/Submit:**

**Don't Forget:**

**Workflow Objective:**

**Phase 1: Initiate:**

**Phase 2: Execute:**

**Phase 3: Monitor:**

**Phase 4: Approve:**

**Phase 5: Wrap Up:**

**Critical Details:**

**Stakeholders:**

**Important Milestones:**

**Quick Contacts:**

| No. | Task: | Purpose: | Completion Date: | Completed? Yes No |
|-----|-------|----------|------------------|-------------------|
| 1 | | | | |
| 2 | | | | |
| 3 | | | | |
| 4 | | | | |
| 5 | | | | |
| 6 | | | | |
| 7 | | | | |
| 8 | | | | |
| 9 | | | | |
| 10 | | | | |
| 11 | | | | |
| 12 | | | | |
| 13 | | | | |
| 14 | | | | |
| 15 | | | | |
| 16 | | | | |
| 17 | | | | |
| 18 | | | | |
| 19 | | | | |
| 20 | | | | |
| 21 | | | | |
| 22 | | | | |
| 23 | | | | |
| 24 | | | | |

|              | Important | Not Important |
| ------------ | --------- | ------------- |
| Urgent       |           |               |
| Non-Urgent   |           |               |

| Important Dates: | Events/ Occasions: | Dress Attire: | Time: |
|---|---|---|---|
| | | | |
| | | | |
| | | | |
| | | | |
| | | | |
| | | | |
| | | | |
| | | | |
| | | | |
| | | | |
| | | | |
| | | | |
| | | | |

**Goals:**
1.
2.
3.

**Tomorrow's Focus:**
1.
2.
3.

**Work Motivation:**
1.
2.
3.

**Personal Motivation:**
1.
2.
3.

*The Blueprint: Project Planner*

# Lingering Thoughts:

**Project 5:**

**Month:**_____ **Week Of:**_____ **Start Date:**_____ **Due Date:**_____

**Priority:**

**Schedule/ Reschedule:**

**Inquire/ Look Into:**

**Log:**

**Print:**

**Email/ Call:**

**Follow Up:**

**Pay/Submit:**

**Don't Forget:**

**Workflow Objective:**

**Phase 1: Initiate:**

**Phase 2: Execute:**

**Phase 3: Monitor:**

**Phase 4: Approve:**

**Phase 5: Wrap Up:**

**Critical Details:**

**Stakeholders:**

**Important Milestones:**

**Quick Contacts:**

| No. | Task: | Purpose: | Completion Date: | Completed? | |
|-----|-------|----------|------------------|------------|----|
| | | | | Yes | No |
| 1 | | | | | |
| 2 | | | | | |
| 3 | | | | | |
| 4 | | | | | |
| 5 | | | | | |
| 6 | | | | | |
| 7 | | | | | |
| 8 | | | | | |
| 9 | | | | | |
| 10 | | | | | |
| 11 | | | | | |
| 12 | | | | | |
| 13 | | | | | |
| 14 | | | | | |
| 15 | | | | | |
| 16 | | | | | |
| 17 | | | | | |
| 18 | | | | | |
| 19 | | | | | |
| 20 | | | | | |
| 21 | | | | | |
| 22 | | | | | |
| 23 | | | | | |
| 24 | | | | | |

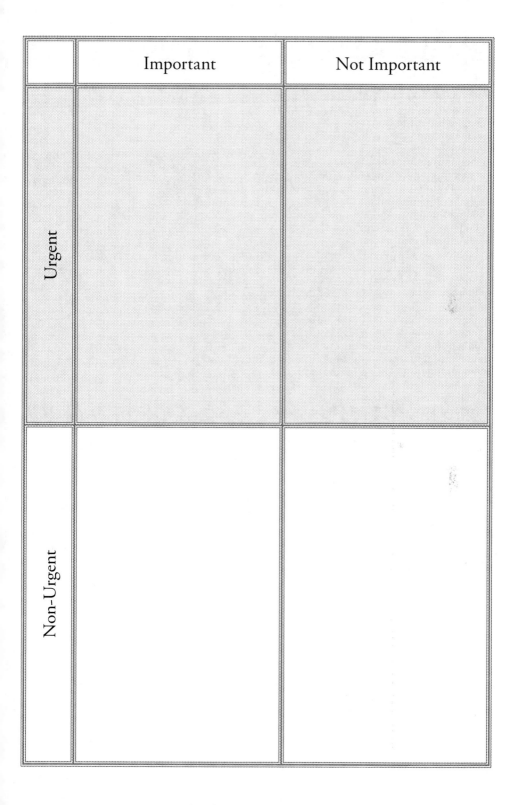

|  | Important | Not Important |
|---|---|---|
| Urgent |  |  |
| Non-Urgent |  |  |

| Important Dates: | Events/ Occasions: | Dress Attire: | Time: |
|---|---|---|---|
|  |  |  |  |
|  |  |  |  |
|  |  |  |  |
|  |  |  |  |
|  |  |  |  |
|  |  |  |  |
|  |  |  |  |
|  |  |  |  |
|  |  |  |  |
|  |  |  |  |
|  |  |  |  |
|  |  |  |  |
|  |  |  |  |
|  |  |  |  |

## Goals:
1.
2.
3.

## Tomorrow's Focus:
1.
2.
3.

## Work Motivation:
1.
2.
3.

## Personal Motivation:
1.
2.
3.

*The Blueprint: Project Planner*

_Lingering Thoughts:_

**Project 6:**

**Month:**_____ **Week Of:**_____ **Start Date:**_____ **Due Date:**_____

**Priority:**

**Schedule/ Reschedule:**

**Inquire/ Look Into:**

**Log:**

**Print:**

**Email/ Call:**

**Follow Up:**

**Pay/Submit:**

**Don't Forget:**

**Workflow Objective:**

**Phase 1: Initiate:**

**Phase 2: Execute:**

**Phase 3: Monitor:**

**Phase 4: Approve:**

**Phase 5: Wrap Up:**

**Critical Details:**

**Stakeholders:**

**Important Milestones:**

**Quick Contacts:**

| No. | Task: | Purpose: | Completion Date: | Completed? | |
|-----|-------|----------|------------------|------------|---|
| | | | | Yes | No |
| 1 | | | | | |
| 2 | | | | | |
| 3 | | | | | |
| 4 | | | | | |
| 5 | | | | | |
| 6 | | | | | |
| 7 | | | | | |
| 8 | | | | | |
| 9 | | | | | |
| 10 | | | | | |
| 11 | | | | | |
| 12 | | | | | |
| 13 | | | | | |
| 14 | | | | | |
| 15 | | | | | |
| 16 | | | | | |
| 17 | | | | | |
| 18 | | | | | |
| 19 | | | | | |
| 20 | | | | | |
| 21 | | | | | |
| 22 | | | | | |
| 23 | | | | | |
| 24 | | | | | |

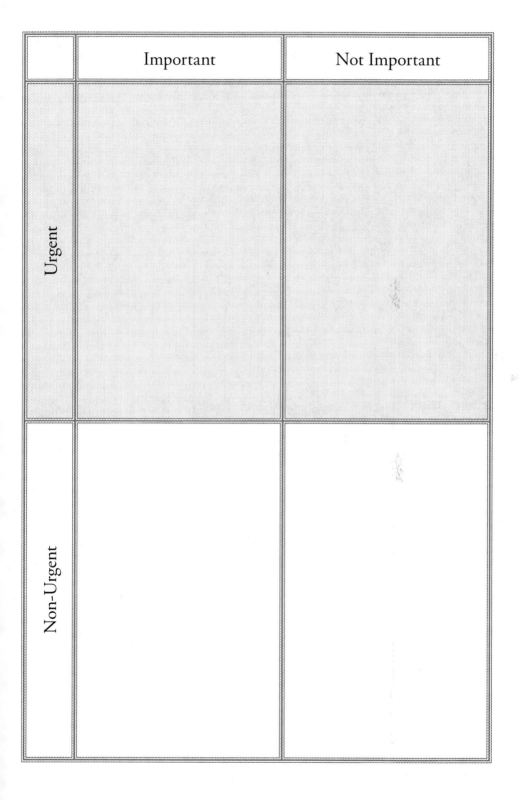

|  | Important | Not Important |
|---|---|---|
| Urgent |  |  |
| Non-Urgent |  |  |

| Important Dates: | Events/ Occasions: | Dress Attire: | Time: |
|---|---|---|---|
| | | | |
| | | | |
| | | | |
| | | | |
| | | | |
| | | | |
| | | | |
| | | | |
| | | | |
| | | | |
| | | | |
| | | | |
| | | | |

## Goals:
1.
2.
3.

## Tomorrow's Focus:
1.
2.
3.

## Work Motivation:
1.
2.
3.

## Personal Motivation:
1.
2.
3.

*Lingering Thoughts:*

**Project 7:**

**Month:**_____ **Week Of:**_____ **Start Date:**_____ **Due Date:**_____

**Priority:**

**Schedule/ Reschedule:**

**Inquire/ Look Into:**

**Log:**

**Print:**

**Email/ Call:**

**Follow Up:**

**Pay/Submit:**

**Don't Forget:**

**Workflow Objective:**

**Phase 1: Initiate:**

**Phase 2: Execute:**

**Phase 3: Monitor:**

**Phase 4: Approve:**

**Phase 5: Wrap Up:**

**Critical Details:**

**Stakeholders:**

**Important Milestones:**

**Quick Contacts:**

| No. | Task: | Purpose: | Completion Date: | Completed? | |
|-----|-------|----------|------------------|------------|---|
| | | | | Yes | No |
| 1 | | | | | |
| 2 | | | | | |
| 3 | | | | | |
| 4 | | | | | |
| 5 | | | | | |
| 6 | | | | | |
| 7 | | | | | |
| 8 | | | | | |
| 9 | | | | | |
| 10 | | | | | |
| 11 | | | | | |
| 12 | | | | | |
| 13 | | | | | |
| 14 | | | | | |
| 15 | | | | | |
| 16 | | | | | |
| 17 | | | | | |
| 18 | | | | | |
| 19 | | | | | |
| 20 | | | | | |
| 21 | | | | | |
| 22 | | | | | |
| 23 | | | | | |
| 24 | | | | | |

*The Blueprint: Project Planner*

|  | Important | Not Important |
|---|---|---|
| **Urgent** | | |
| **Non-Urgent** | | |

| Important Dates: | Events/ Occasions: | Dress Attire: | Time: |
|---|---|---|---|
| | | | |
| | | | |
| | | | |
| | | | |
| | | | |
| | | | |
| | | | |
| | | | |
| | | | |
| | | | |
| | | | |
| | | | |

**Goals:**

1.
2.
3.

**Tomorrow's Focus:**

1.
2.
3.

**Work Motivation:**

1.
2.
3.

**Personal Motivation:**

1.
2.
3.

*Lingering Thoughts:*

**Project 8:**

Month:_____ Week Of:_____ Start Date:_____ Due Date:_____

**Priority:**

**Schedule/ Reschedule:**

**Inquire/ Look Into:**

**Log:**

**Print:**

**Email/ Call:**

**Follow Up:**

**Pay/Submit:**

**Don't Forget:**

*The Blueprint: Project Planner*

**Workflow Objective:**

**Phase 1: Initiate:**

**Phase 2: Execute:**

**Phase 3: Monitor:**

**Phase 4: Approve:**

**Phase 5: Wrap Up:**

**Critical Details:**

**Stakeholders:**

**Important Milestones:**

**Quick Contacts:**

| No. | Task: | Purpose: | Completion Date: | Completed? | |
|-----|-------|----------|------------------|------------|---|
| | | | | Yes | No |
| 1 | | | | | |
| 2 | | | | | |
| 3 | | | | | |
| 4 | | | | | |
| 5 | | | | | |
| 6 | | | | | |
| 7 | | | | | |
| 8 | | | | | |
| 9 | | | | | |
| 10 | | | | | |
| 11 | | | | | |
| 12 | | | | | |
| 13 | | | | | |
| 14 | | | | | |
| 15 | | | | | |
| 16 | | | | | |
| 17 | | | | | |
| 18 | | | | | |
| 19 | | | | | |
| 20 | | | | | |
| 21 | | | | | |
| 22 | | | | | |
| 23 | | | | | |
| 24 | | | | | |

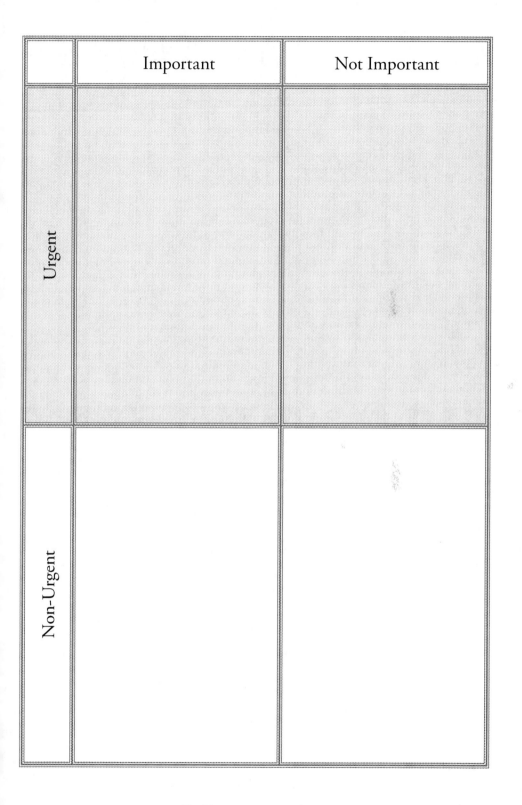

|  | Important | Not Important |
|---|---|---|
| Urgent | | |
| Non-Urgent | | |

| Important Dates: | Events/ Occasions: | Dress Attire: | Time: |
|---|---|---|---|
|  |  |  |  |
|  |  |  |  |
|  |  |  |  |
|  |  |  |  |
|  |  |  |  |
|  |  |  |  |
|  |  |  |  |
|  |  |  |  |
|  |  |  |  |
|  |  |  |  |
|  |  |  |  |
|  |  |  |  |
|  |  |  |  |

**Goals:**

1.
2.
3.

**Tomorrow's Focus:**

1.
2.
3.

**Work Motivation:**

1.
2.
3.

**Personal Motivation:**

1.
2.
3.

*The Blueprint: Project Planner*

# Lingering Thoughts:

**Project 9:**

**Month:**_____ **Week Of:**_____ **Start Date:**_____ **Due Date:**_____

**Priority:**

**Schedule/ Reschedule:**

**Inquire/ Look Into:**

**Log:**

**Print:**

**Email/ Call:**

**Follow Up:**

**Pay/Submit:**

**Don't Forget:**

**Workflow Objective:**

**Phase 1: Initiate:**

**Phase 2: Execute:**

**Phase 3: Monitor:**

**Phase 4: Approve:**

**Phase 5: Wrap Up:**

**Critical Details:**

**Stakeholders:**

**Important Milestones:**

**Quick Contacts:**

| No. | Task: | Purpose: | Completion Date: | Completed? Yes No |
|-----|-------|----------|------------------|:---:|
| 1 | | | | |
| 2 | | | | |
| 3 | | | | |
| 4 | | | | |
| 5 | | | | |
| 6 | | | | |
| 7 | | | | |
| 8 | | | | |
| 9 | | | | |
| 10 | | | | |
| 11 | | | | |
| 12 | | | | |
| 13 | | | | |
| 14 | | | | |
| 15 | | | | |
| 16 | | | | |
| 17 | | | | |
| 18 | | | | |
| 19 | | | | |
| 20 | | | | |
| 21 | | | | |
| 22 | | | | |
| 23 | | | | |
| 24 | | | | |

*The Blueprint: Project Planner*

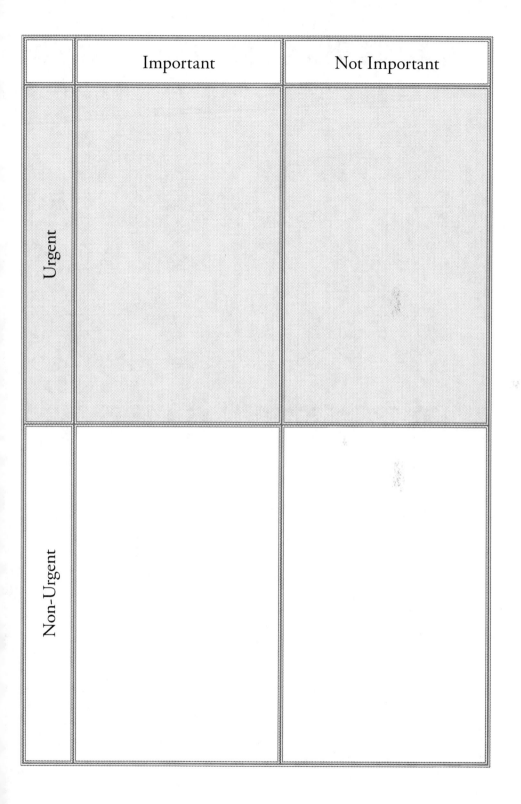

|  | Important | Not Important |
|---|---|---|
| **Urgent** |  |  |
| **Non-Urgent** |  |  |

| Important Dates: | Events/ Occasions: | Dress Attire: | Time: |
|---|---|---|---|
| | | | |
| | | | |
| | | | |
| | | | |
| | | | |
| | | | |
| | | | |
| | | | |
| | | | |
| | | | |
| | | | |
| | | | |
| | | | |
| | | | |

| Goals: |
|---|
| 1. |
| 2. |
| 3. |
| |

**Tomorrow's Focus:**

| |
|---|
| 1. |
| 2. |
| 3. |
| |

**Work Motivation:**

| |
|---|
| 1. |
| 2. |
| 3. |
| |

**Personal Motivation:**

| |
|---|
| 1. |
| 2. |
| 3. |
| |

**Project 10:**

**Month:**_____ **Week Of:**_____ **Start Date:**_____ **Due Date:**_____

**Priority:**

**Schedule/ Reschedule:**

**Inquire/ Look Into:**

**Log:**

**Print:**

**Email/ Call:**

**Follow Up:**

**Pay/Submit:**

**Don't Forget:**

**Workflow Objective:**

**Phase 1: Initiate:**

**Phase 2: Execute:**

**Phase 3: Monitor:**

**Phase 4: Approve:**

**Phase 5: Wrap Up:**

**Critical Details:**

**Stakeholders:**

**Important Milestones:**

**Quick Contacts:**

| No. | Task: | Purpose: | Completion Date: | Completed? Yes  No |
|-----|-------|----------|------------------|-----|
| 1 | | | | |
| 2 | | | | |
| 3 | | | | |
| 4 | | | | |
| 5 | | | | |
| 6 | | | | |
| 7 | | | | |
| 8 | | | | |
| 9 | | | | |
| 10 | | | | |
| 11 | | | | |
| 12 | | | | |
| 13 | | | | |
| 14 | | | | |
| 15 | | | | |
| 16 | | | | |
| 17 | | | | |
| 18 | | | | |
| 19 | | | | |
| 20 | | | | |
| 21 | | | | |
| 22 | | | | |
| 23 | | | | |
| 24 | | | | |

|            | Important | Not Important |
| ---------- | --------- | ------------- |
| Urgent     |           |               |
| Non-Urgent |           |               |

| Important Dates: | Events/ Occasions: | Dress Attire: | Time: |
|---|---|---|---|
| | | | |
| | | | |
| | | | |
| | | | |
| | | | |
| | | | |
| | | | |
| | | | |
| | | | |
| | | | |
| | | | |
| | | | |
| | | | |
| | | | |
| | | | |

## Goals:
1.
2.
3.

## Tomorrow's Focus:
1.
2.
3.

## Work Motivation:
1.
2.
3.

## Personal Motivation:
1.
2.
3.

*Lingering Thoughts:*

**Project 11:**

**Month:**_____ **Week Of:**_____ **Start Date:**_____ **Due Date:**_____

**Priority:**

**Schedule/ Reschedule:**

**Inquire/ Look Into:**

**Log:**

**Print:**

**Email/ Call:**

**Follow Up:**

**Pay/Submit:**

**Don't Forget:**

**Workflow Objective:**

**Phase 1: Initiate:**

**Phase 2: Execute:**

**Phase 3: Monitor:**

**Phase 4: Approve:**

**Phase 5: Wrap Up:**

**Critical Details:**

**Stakeholders:**

**Important Milestones:**

**Quick Contacts:**

| No. | Task: | Purpose: | Completion Date: | Completed? | |
|-----|-------|----------|------------------|------------|---|
| | | | | Yes | No |
| 1 | | | | | |
| 2 | | | | | |
| 3 | | | | | |
| 4 | | | | | |
| 5 | | | | | |
| 6 | | | | | |
| 7 | | | | | |
| 8 | | | | | |
| 9 | | | | | |
| 10 | | | | | |
| 11 | | | | | |
| 12 | | | | | |
| 13 | | | | | |
| 14 | | | | | |
| 15 | | | | | |
| 16 | | | | | |
| 17 | | | | | |
| 18 | | | | | |
| 19 | | | | | |
| 20 | | | | | |
| 21 | | | | | |
| 22 | | | | | |
| 23 | | | | | |
| 24 | | | | | |

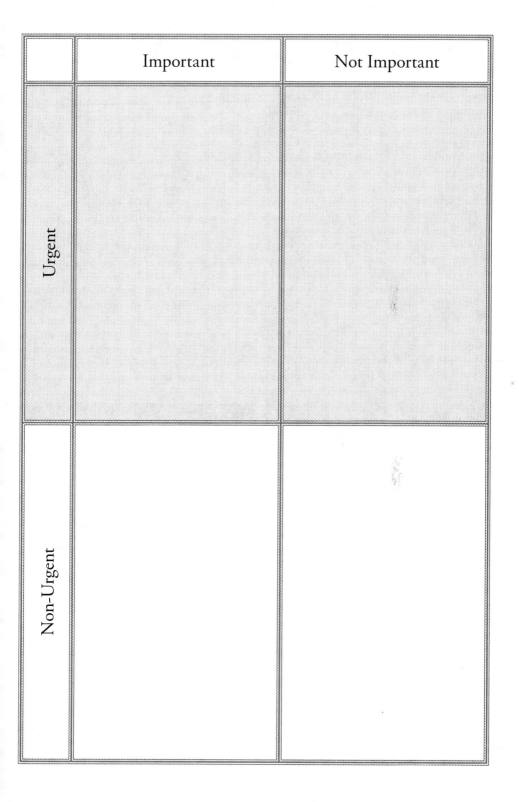

|  | Important | Not Important |
|---|---|---|
| **Urgent** |  |  |
| **Non-Urgent** |  |  |

| Important Dates: | Events/ Occasions: | Dress Attire: | Time: |
|---|---|---|---|
| | | | |
| | | | |
| | | | |
| | | | |
| | | | |
| | | | |
| | | | |
| | | | |
| | | | |
| | | | |
| | | | |
| | | | |

**Goals:**

1.

2.

3.

**Tomorrow's Focus:**

1.

2.

3.

**Work Motivation:**

1.

2.

3.

**Personal Motivation:**

1.

2.

3.

# *Lingering Thoughts:*

**Project 12:**

**Month:**_____ **Week Of:**_____ **Start Date:**_____ **Due Date:**_____

**Priority:**

**Schedule/ Reschedule:**

**Inquire/ Look Into:**

**Log:**

**Print:**

**Email/ Call:**

**Follow Up:**

**Pay/Submit:**

**Don't Forget:**

**Workflow Objective:**

**Phase 1: Initiate:**

**Phase 2: Execute:**

**Phase 3: Monitor:**

**Phase 4: Approve:**

**Phase 5: Wrap Up:**

**Critical Details:**

**Stakeholders:**

**Important Milestones:**

**Quick Contacts:**

| No. | Task: | Purpose: | Completion Date: | Completed? | |
|-----|-------|----------|------------------|:---:|:---:|
| | | | | Yes | No |
| 1 | | | | | |
| 2 | | | | | |
| 3 | | | | | |
| 4 | | | | | |
| 5 | | | | | |
| 6 | | | | | |
| 7 | | | | | |
| 8 | | | | | |
| 9 | | | | | |
| 10 | | | | | |
| 11 | | | | | |
| 12 | | | | | |
| 13 | | | | | |
| 14 | | | | | |
| 15 | | | | | |
| 16 | | | | | |
| 17 | | | | | |
| 18 | | | | | |
| 19 | | | | | |
| 20 | | | | | |
| 21 | | | | | |
| 22 | | | | | |
| 23 | | | | | |
| 24 | | | | | |

*The Blueprint: Project Planner*

|  | Important | Not Important |
|---|---|---|
| **Urgent** | | |
| **Non-Urgent** | | |

| Important Dates: | Events/ Occasions: | Dress Attire: | Time: |
|---|---|---|---|
|  |  |  |  |
|  |  |  |  |
|  |  |  |  |
|  |  |  |  |
|  |  |  |  |
|  |  |  |  |
|  |  |  |  |
|  |  |  |  |
|  |  |  |  |
|  |  |  |  |
|  |  |  |  |
|  |  |  |  |

## Goals:
1.
2.
3.

## Tomorrow's Focus:
1.
2.
3.

## Work Motivation:
1.
2.
3.

## Personal Motivation:
1.
2.
3.

*The Blueprint: Project Planner*

*Lingering Thoughts:*

**Project 13:**

**Month:**_____ **Week Of:**_____ **Start Date:**_____ **Due Date:**_____

**Priority:**

**Schedule/ Reschedule:**

**Inquire/ Look Into:**

**Log:**

**Print:**

**Email/ Call:**

**Follow Up:**

**Pay/Submit:**

**Don't Forget:**

**Workflow Objective:**

**Phase 1: Initiate:**

**Phase 2: Execute:**

**Phase 3: Monitor:**

**Phase 4: Approve:**

**Phase 5: Wrap Up:**

**Critical Details:**

**Stakeholders:**

**Important Milestones:**

**Quick Contacts:**

| No. | Task: | Purpose: | Completion Date: | Completed? | |
|-----|-------|----------|------------------|------------|----|
| | | | | Yes | No |
| 1 | | | | | |
| 2 | | | | | |
| 3 | | | | | |
| 4 | | | | | |
| 5 | | | | | |
| 6 | | | | | |
| 7 | | | | | |
| 8 | | | | | |
| 9 | | | | | |
| 10 | | | | | |
| 11 | | | | | |
| 12 | | | | | |
| 13 | | | | | |
| 14 | | | | | |
| 15 | | | | | |
| 16 | | | | | |
| 17 | | | | | |
| 18 | | | | | |
| 19 | | | | | |
| 20 | | | | | |
| 21 | | | | | |
| 22 | | | | | |
| 23 | | | | | |
| 24 | | | | | |

*The Blueprint: Project Planner*

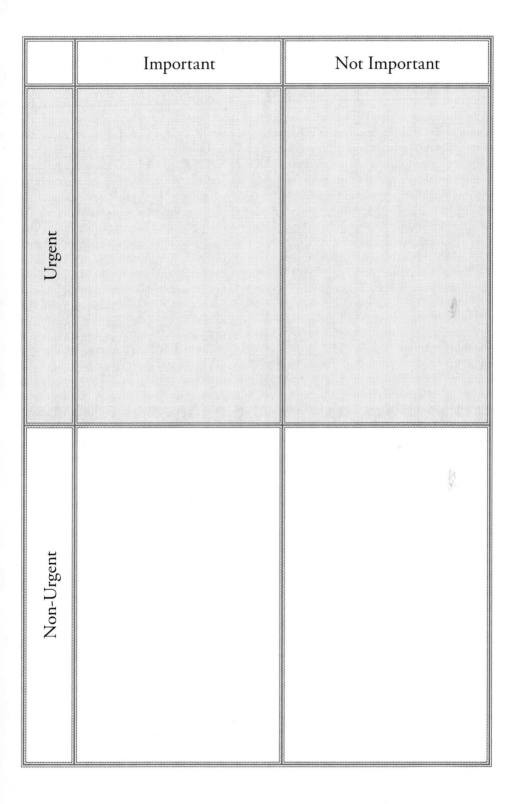

|  | Important | Not Important |
|---|---|---|
| Urgent | | |
| Non-Urgent | | |

| Important Dates: | Events/ Occasions: | Dress Attire: | Time: |
| --- | --- | --- | --- |
|  |  |  |  |
|  |  |  |  |
|  |  |  |  |
|  |  |  |  |
|  |  |  |  |
|  |  |  |  |
|  |  |  |  |
|  |  |  |  |
|  |  |  |  |
|  |  |  |  |
|  |  |  |  |
|  |  |  |  |

**Goals:**

1.

2.

3.

**Tomorrow's Focus:**

1.

2.

3.

**Work Motivation:**

1.

2.

3.

**Personal Motivation:**

1.

2.

3.

*Lingering Thoughts:*

**Project 14:**

**Month:_____ Week Of:_____ Start Date:_____ Due Date:_____**

**Priority:**

**Schedule/ Reschedule:**

**Inquire/ Look Into:**

**Log:**

**Print:**

**Email/ Call:**

**Follow Up:**

**Pay/Submit:**

**Don't Forget:**

**Workflow Objective:**

**Phase 1: Initiate:**

**Phase 2: Execute:**

**Phase 3: Monitor:**

**Phase 4: Approve:**

**Phase 5: Wrap Up:**

**Critical Details:**

**Stakeholders:**

**Important Milestones:**

**Quick Contacts:**

| No. | Task: | Purpose: | Completion Date: | Completed? | |
|-----|-------|----------|------------------|------------|---|
| | | | | Yes | No |
| 1 | | | | | |
| 2 | | | | | |
| 3 | | | | | |
| 4 | | | | | |
| 5 | | | | | |
| 6 | | | | | |
| 7 | | | | | |
| 8 | | | | | |
| 9 | | | | | |
| 10 | | | | | |
| 11 | | | | | |
| 12 | | | | | |
| 13 | | | | | |
| 14 | | | | | |
| 15 | | | | | |
| 16 | | | | | |
| 17 | | | | | |
| 18 | | | | | |
| 19 | | | | | |
| 20 | | | | | |
| 21 | | | | | |
| 22 | | | | | |
| 23 | | | | | |
| 24 | | | | | |

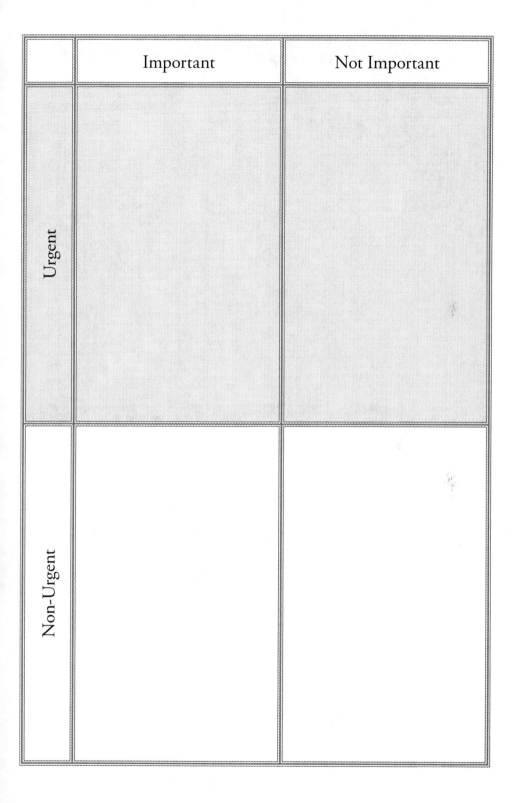

|  | Important | Not Important |
|---|---|---|
| Urgent | | |
| Non-Urgent | | |

| Important Dates: | Events/ Occasions: | Dress Attire: | Time: |
| --- | --- | --- | --- |
| | | | |
| | | | |
| | | | |
| | | | |
| | | | |
| | | | |
| | | | |
| | | | |
| | | | |
| | | | |
| | | | |
| | | | |
| | | | |

## Goals:
1.
2.
3.

## Tomorrow's Focus:
1.
2.
3.

## Work Motivation:
1.
2.
3.

## Personal Motivation:
1.
2.
3.

*Lingering Thoughts:*

**Project 15:**

Month:_____ Week Of:_____ Start Date:_____ Due Date:_____

**Priority:**

**Schedule/ Reschedule:**

**Inquire/ Look Into:**

**Log:**

**Print:**

**Email/ Call:**

**Follow Up:**

**Pay/Submit:**

**Don't Forget:**

**Workflow Objective:**

**Phase 1: Initiate:**

**Phase 2: Execute:**

**Phase 3: Monitor:**

**Phase 4: Approve:**

**Phase 5: Wrap Up:**

**Critical Details:**

**Stakeholders:**

**Important Milestones:**

**Quick Contacts:**

| No. | Task: | Purpose: | Completion Date: | Completed? Yes No |
|---|---|---|---|---|
| 1 | | | | |
| 2 | | | | |
| 3 | | | | |
| 4 | | | | |
| 5 | | | | |
| 6 | | | | |
| 7 | | | | |
| 8 | | | | |
| 9 | | | | |
| 10 | | | | |
| 11 | | | | |
| 12 | | | | |
| 13 | | | | |
| 14 | | | | |
| 15 | | | | |
| 16 | | | | |
| 17 | | | | |
| 18 | | | | |
| 19 | | | | |
| 20 | | | | |
| 21 | | | | |
| 22 | | | | |
| 23 | | | | |
| 24 | | | | |

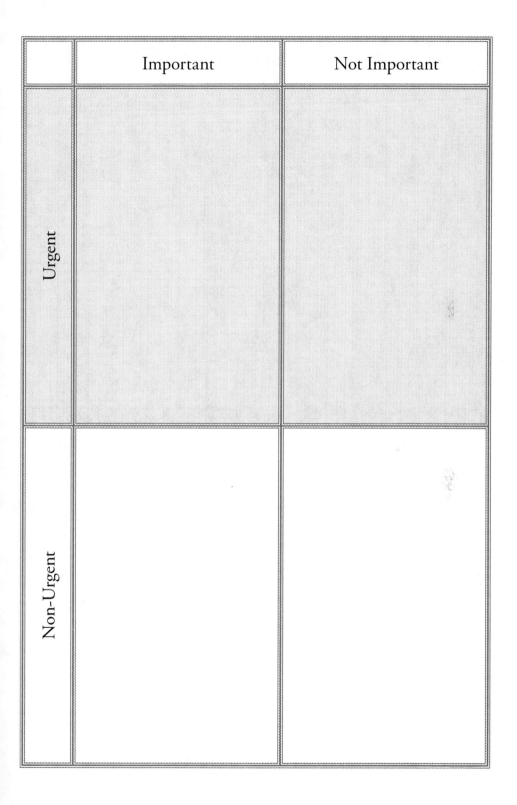

|  | Important | Not Important |
|---|---|---|
| Urgent | | |
| Non-Urgent | | |

| Important Dates: | Events/ Occasions: | Dress Attire: | Time: |
|---|---|---|---|
|  |  |  |  |
|  |  |  |  |
|  |  |  |  |
|  |  |  |  |
|  |  |  |  |
|  |  |  |  |
|  |  |  |  |
|  |  |  |  |
|  |  |  |  |
|  |  |  |  |
|  |  |  |  |
|  |  |  |  |
|  |  |  |  |
|  |  |  |  |

**Goals:**
1.
2.
3.

**Tomorrow's Focus:**
1.
2.
3.

**Work Motivation:**
1.
2.
3.

**Personal Motivation:**
1.
2.
3.

# Lingering Thoughts:

**Project 16:**

**Month:**_____ **Week Of:**_____ **Start Date:**_____ **Due Date:**_____

**Priority:**

**Schedule/ Reschedule:**

**Inquire/ Look Into:**

**Log:**

**Print:**

**Email/ Call:**

**Follow Up:**

**Pay/Submit:**

**Don't Forget:**

**Workflow Objective:**

**Phase 1: Initiate:**

**Phase 2: Execute:**

**Phase 3: Monitor:**

**Phase 4: Approve:**

**Phase 5: Wrap Up:**

**Critical Details:**

**Stakeholders:**

**Important Milestones:**

**Quick Contacts:**

| No. | Task: | Purpose: | Completion Date: | Completed? Yes  No |
|-----|-------|----------|------------------|---------|
| 1 | | | | |
| 2 | | | | |
| 3 | | | | |
| 4 | | | | |
| 5 | | | | |
| 6 | | | | |
| 7 | | | | |
| 8 | | | | |
| 9 | | | | |
| 10 | | | | |
| 11 | | | | |
| 12 | | | | |
| 13 | | | | |
| 14 | | | | |
| 15 | | | | |
| 16 | | | | |
| 17 | | | | |
| 18 | | | | |
| 19 | | | | |
| 20 | | | | |
| 21 | | | | |
| 22 | | | | |
| 23 | | | | |
| 24 | | | | |

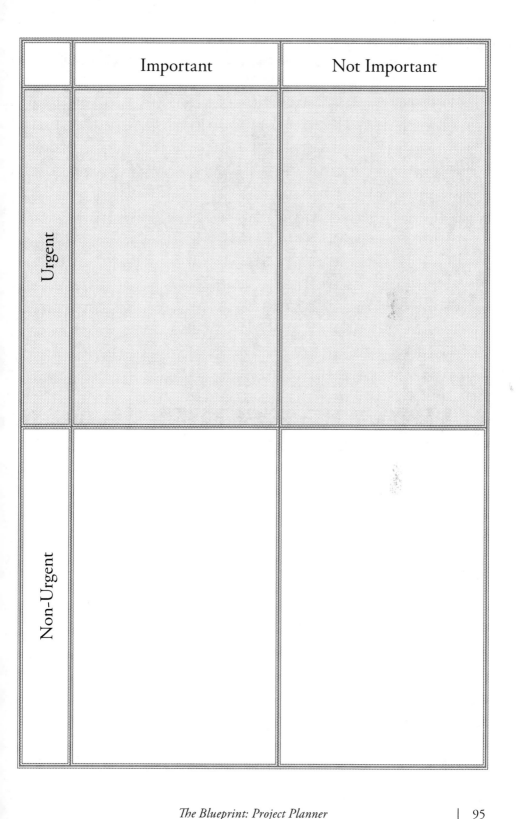

|  | Important | Not Important |
|---|---|---|
| **Urgent** | | |
| **Non-Urgent** | | |

| Important Dates: | Events/ Occasions: | Dress Attire: | Time: |
| --- | --- | --- | --- |
| | | | |
| | | | |
| | | | |
| | | | |
| | | | |
| | | | |
| | | | |
| | | | |
| | | | |
| | | | |
| | | | |

## Goals:
1.
2.
3.

## Tomorrow's Focus:
1.
2.
3.

## Work Motivation:
1.
2.
3.

## Personal Motivation:
1.
2.
3.

*Lingering Thoughts:*

**Project 17:**

**Month:**_____ **Week Of:**_____ **Start Date:**_____ **Due Date:**_____

**Priority:**

**Schedule/ Reschedule:**

**Inquire/ Look Into:**

**Log:**

**Print:**

**Email/ Call:**

**Follow Up:**

**Pay/Submit:**

**Don't Forget:**

**Workflow Objective:**

**Phase 1: Initiate:**

**Phase 2: Execute:**

**Phase 3: Monitor:**

**Phase 4: Approve:**

**Phase 5: Wrap Up:**

**Critical Details:**

**Stakeholders:**

**Important Milestones:**

**Quick Contacts:**

| No. | Task: | Purpose: | Completion Date: | Completed? Yes No |
|---|---|---|---|---|
| 1 | | | | |
| 2 | | | | |
| 3 | | | | |
| 4 | | | | |
| 5 | | | | |
| 6 | | | | |
| 7 | | | | |
| 8 | | | | |
| 9 | | | | |
| 10 | | | | |
| 11 | | | | |
| 12 | | | | |
| 13 | | | | |
| 14 | | | | |
| 15 | | | | |
| 16 | | | | |
| 17 | | | | |
| 18 | | | | |
| 19 | | | | |
| 20 | | | | |
| 21 | | | | |
| 22 | | | | |
| 23 | | | | |
| 24 | | | | |

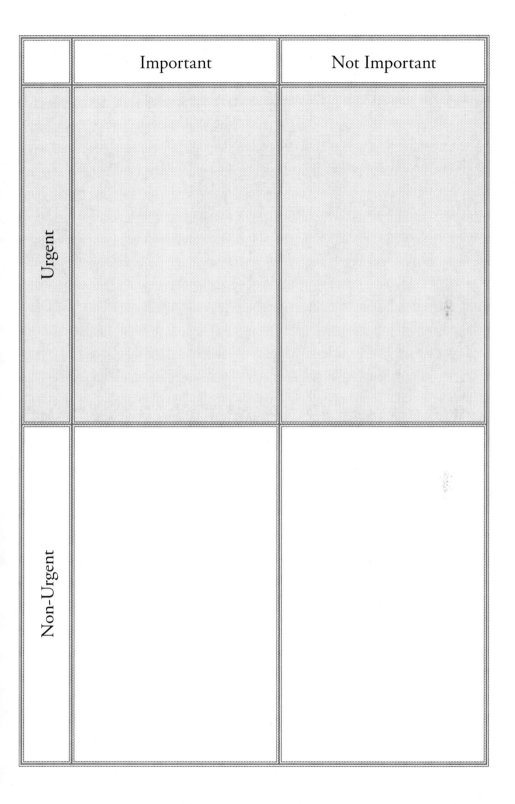

|  | Important | Not Important |
|---|---|---|
| Urgent |  |  |
| Non-Urgent |  |  |

| Important Dates: | Events/ Occasions: | Dress Attire: | Time: |
|---|---|---|---|
| | | | |
| | | | |
| | | | |
| | | | |
| | | | |
| | | | |
| | | | |
| | | | |
| | | | |
| | | | |
| | | | |
| | | | |

**Goals:**

1.
2.
3.

**Tomorrow's Focus:**

1.
2.
3.

**Work Motivation:**

1.
2.
3.

**Personal Motivation:**

1.
2.
3.

*Lingering Thoughts:*

**Project 18:**

**Month:**_____ **Week Of:**_____ **Start Date:**_____ **Due Date:**_____

**Priority:**

**Schedule/ Reschedule:**

**Inquire/ Look Into:**

**Log:**

**Print:**

**Email/ Call:**

**Follow Up:**

**Pay/Submit:**

**Don't Forget:**

**Workflow Objective:**

**Phase 1: Initiate:**

**Phase 2: Execute:**

**Phase 3: Monitor:**

**Phase 4: Approve:**

**Phase 5: Wrap Up:**

**Critical Details:**

**Stakeholders:**

**Important Milestones:**

**Quick Contacts:**

| No. | Task: | Purpose: | Completion Date: | Completed? Yes No |
|-----|-------|----------|------------------|-----|
| 1 | | | | |
| 2 | | | | |
| 3 | | | | |
| 4 | | | | |
| 5 | | | | |
| 6 | | | | |
| 7 | | | | |
| 8 | | | | |
| 9 | | | | |
| 10 | | | | |
| 11 | | | | |
| 12 | | | | |
| 13 | | | | |
| 14 | | | | |
| 15 | | | | |
| 16 | | | | |
| 17 | | | | |
| 18 | | | | |
| 19 | | | | |
| 20 | | | | |
| 21 | | | | |
| 22 | | | | |
| 23 | | | | |
| 24 | | | | |

|  | Important | Not Important |
|---|---|---|
| **Urgent** | | |
| **Non-Urgent** | | |

| Important Dates: | Events/ Occasions: | Dress Attire: | Time: |
|---|---|---|---|
| | | | |
| | | | |
| | | | |
| | | | |
| | | | |
| | | | |
| | | | |
| | | | |
| | | | |
| | | | |
| | | | |
| | | | |
| | | | |
| | | | |

## Goals:
1.
2.
3.

## Tomorrow's Focus:
1.
2.
3.

## Work Motivation:
1.
2.
3.

## Personal Motivation:
1.
2.
3.

*Lingering Thoughts:*

**Project 19:**

**Month:**_____ **Week Of:**_____ **Start Date:**_____ **Due Date:**_____

**Priority:**

**Schedule/ Reschedule:**

**Inquire/ Look Into:**

**Log:**

**Print:**

**Email/ Call:**

**Follow Up:**

**Pay/Submit:**

**Don't Forget:**

**Workflow Objective:**

**Phase 1: Initiate:**

**Phase 2: Execute:**

**Phase 3: Monitor:**

**Phase 4: Approve:**

**Phase 5: Wrap Up:**

**Critical Details:**

**Stakeholders:**

**Important Milestones:**

**Quick Contacts:**

| No. | Task: | Purpose: | Completion Date: | Completed? Yes No | |
|---|---|---|---|---|---|
| 1 | | | | | |
| 2 | | | | | |
| 3 | | | | | |
| 4 | | | | | |
| 5 | | | | | |
| 6 | | | | | |
| 7 | | | | | |
| 8 | | | | | |
| 9 | | | | | |
| 10 | | | | | |
| 11 | | | | | |
| 12 | | | | | |
| 13 | | | | | |
| 14 | | | | | |
| 15 | | | | | |
| 16 | | | | | |
| 17 | | | | | |
| 18 | | | | | |
| 19 | | | | | |
| 20 | | | | | |
| 21 | | | | | |
| 22 | | | | | |
| 23 | | | | | |
| 24 | | | | | |

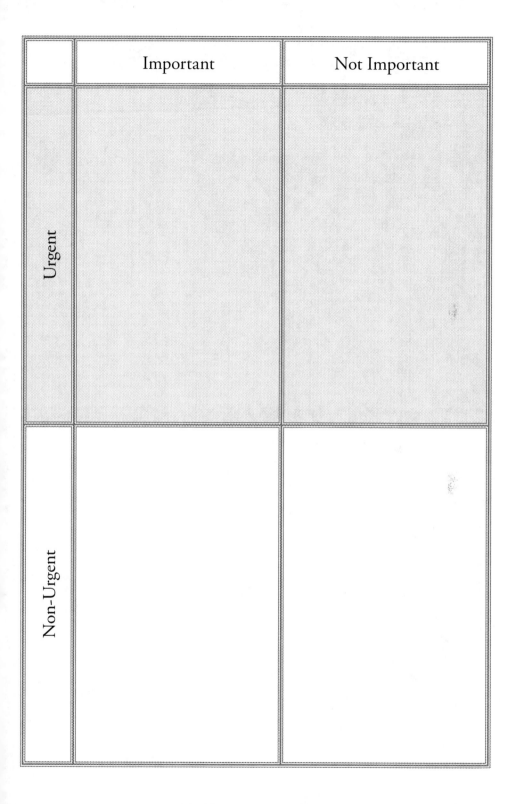

|  | Important | Not Important |
|---|---|---|
| **Urgent** | | |
| **Non-Urgent** | | |

| Important Dates: | Events/ Occasions: | Dress Attire: | Time: |
|---|---|---|---|
| | | | |
| | | | |
| | | | |
| | | | |
| | | | |
| | | | |
| | | | |
| | | | |
| | | | |
| | | | |
| | | | |
| | | | |
| | | | |
| | | | |

**Goals:**

1.
2.
3.

**Tomorrow's Focus:**

1.
2.
3.

**Work Motivation:**

1.
2.
3.

**Personal Motivation:**

1.
2.
3.

_Lingering Thoughts:_

**Project 20:**

**Month:**_____ **Week Of:**_____ **Start Date:**_____ **Due Date:**_____

**Priority:**

**Schedule/ Reschedule:**

**Inquire/ Look Into:**

**Log:**

**Print:**

**Email/ Call:**

**Follow Up:**

**Pay/Submit:**

**Don't Forget:**

**Workflow Objective:**

**Phase 1: Initiate:**

**Phase 2: Execute:**

**Phase 3: Monitor:**

**Phase 4: Approve:**

**Phase 5: Wrap Up:**

**Critical Details:**

**Stakeholders:**

**Important Milestones:**

**Quick Contacts:**

| No. | Task: | Purpose: | Completion Date: | Completed? | |
|-----|-------|----------|------------------|------------|----|
| | | | | Yes | No |
| 1 | | | | | |
| 2 | | | | | |
| 3 | | | | | |
| 4 | | | | | |
| 5 | | | | | |
| 6 | | | | | |
| 7 | | | | | |
| 8 | | | | | |
| 9 | | | | | |
| 10 | | | | | |
| 11 | | | | | |
| 12 | | | | | |
| 13 | | | | | |
| 14 | | | | | |
| 15 | | | | | |
| 16 | | | | | |
| 17 | | | | | |
| 18 | | | | | |
| 19 | | | | | |
| 20 | | | | | |
| 21 | | | | | |
| 22 | | | | | |
| 23 | | | | | |
| 24 | | | | | |

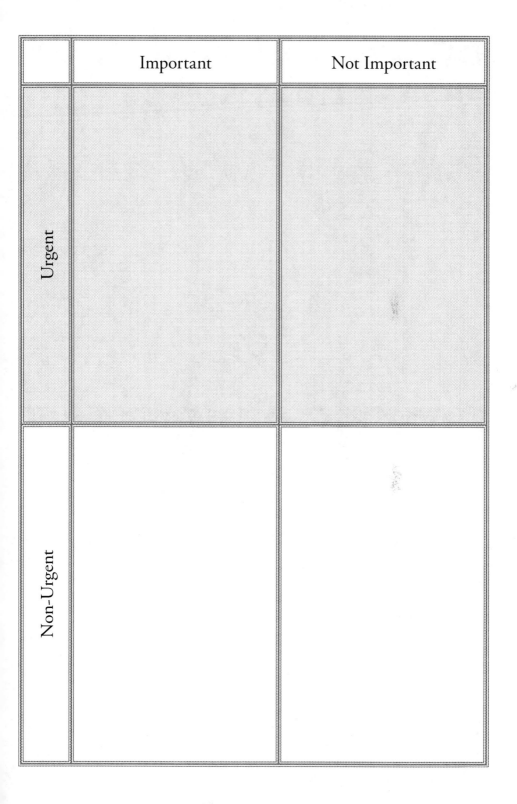

|              | Important | Not Important |
|--------------|-----------|---------------|
| Urgent       |           |               |
| Non-Urgent   |           |               |

| Important Dates: | Events/ Occasions: | Dress Attire: | Time: |
|---|---|---|---|
|  |  |  |  |
|  |  |  |  |
|  |  |  |  |
|  |  |  |  |
|  |  |  |  |
|  |  |  |  |
|  |  |  |  |
|  |  |  |  |
|  |  |  |  |
|  |  |  |  |
|  |  |  |  |
|  |  |  |  |
|  |  |  |  |

**Goals:**
1.
2.
3.

**Tomorrow's Focus:**
1.
2.
3.

**Work Motivation:**
1.
2.
3.

**Personal Motivation:**
1.
2.
3.

*The Blueprint: Project Planner*

Lingering Thoughts:

**Project 21:**

Month:_____ Week Of:_____ Start Date:_____ Due Date:_____

**Priority:**

**Schedule/ Reschedule:**

**Inquire/ Look Into:**

**Log:**

**Print:**

**Email/ Call:**

**Follow Up:**

**Pay/Submit:**

**Don't Forget:**

**Workflow Objective:**

**Phase 1: Initiate:**

**Phase 2: Execute:**

**Phase 3: Monitor:**

**Phase 4: Approve:**

**Phase 5: Wrap Up:**

**Critical Details:**

**Stakeholders:**

**Important Milestones:**

**Quick Contacts:**

| No. | Task: | Purpose: | Completion Date: | Completed? Yes No |
|---|---|---|---|---|
| 1 | | | | |
| 2 | | | | |
| 3 | | | | |
| 4 | | | | |
| 5 | | | | |
| 6 | | | | |
| 7 | | | | |
| 8 | | | | |
| 9 | | | | |
| 10 | | | | |
| 11 | | | | |
| 12 | | | | |
| 13 | | | | |
| 14 | | | | |
| 15 | | | | |
| 16 | | | | |
| 17 | | | | |
| 18 | | | | |
| 19 | | | | |
| 20 | | | | |
| 21 | | | | |
| 22 | | | | |
| 23 | | | | |
| 24 | | | | |

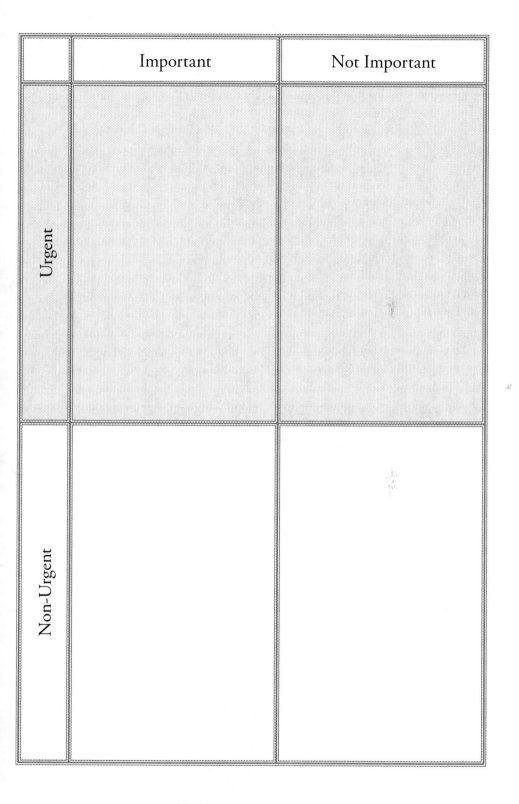

|  | Important | Not Important |
|---|---|---|
| Urgent | | |
| Non-Urgent | | |

| Important Dates: | Events/ Occasions: | Dress Attire: | Time: |
|---|---|---|---|
| | | | |
| | | | |
| | | | |
| | | | |
| | | | |
| | | | |
| | | | |
| | | | |
| | | | |
| | | | |
| | | | |
| | | | |

## Goals:
1.
2.
3.

## Tomorrow's Focus:
1.
2.
3.

## Work Motivation:
1.
2.
3.

## Personal Motivation:
1.
2.
3.

*Lingering Thoughts:*

**Project 22:**

**Month:**_____ **Week Of:**_____ **Start Date:**_____ **Due Date:**_____

**Priority:**

**Schedule/ Reschedule:**

**Inquire/ Look Into:**

**Log:**

**Print:**

**Email/ Call:**

**Follow Up:**

**Pay/Submit:**

**Don't Forget:**

**Workflow Objective:**

**Phase 1: Initiate:**

**Phase 2: Execute:**

**Phase 3: Monitor:**

**Phase 4: Approve:**

**Phase 5: Wrap Up:**

**Critical Details:**

**Stakeholders:**

**Important Milestones:**

**Quick Contacts:**

| No. | Task: | Purpose: | Completion Date: | Completed? Yes No |
|-----|-------|----------|------------------|-------------------|
| 1 | | | | |
| 2 | | | | |
| 3 | | | | |
| 4 | | | | |
| 5 | | | | |
| 6 | | | | |
| 7 | | | | |
| 8 | | | | |
| 9 | | | | |
| 10 | | | | |
| 11 | | | | |
| 12 | | | | |
| 13 | | | | |
| 14 | | | | |
| 15 | | | | |
| 16 | | | | |
| 17 | | | | |
| 18 | | | | |
| 19 | | | | |
| 20 | | | | |
| 21 | | | | |
| 22 | | | | |
| 23 | | | | |
| 24 | | | | |

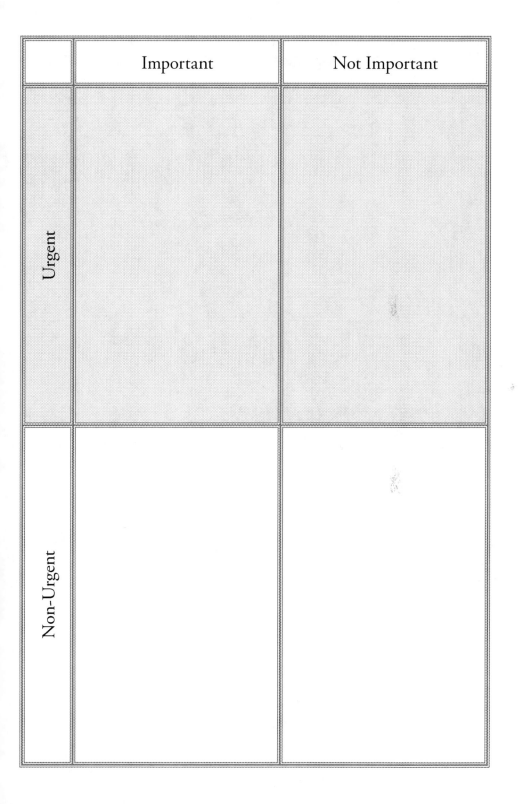

|  | Important | Not Important |
|---|---|---|
| Urgent | | |
| Non-Urgent | | |

| Important Dates: | Events/ Occasions: | Dress Attire: | Time: |
|---|---|---|---|
| | | | |
| | | | |
| | | | |
| | | | |
| | | | |
| | | | |
| | | | |
| | | | |
| | | | |
| | | | |
| | | | |
| | | | |

## Goals:
1.
2.
3.



## Tomorrow's Focus:
1.
2.
3.

## Work Motivation:
1.
2.
3.

## Personal Motivation:
1.
2.
3.

_Lingering Thoughts:_

**Project 23:**

**Month:**_____ **Week Of:**_____ **Start Date:**_____ **Due Date:**_____

**Priority:**

**Schedule/ Reschedule:**

**Inquire/ Look Into:**

**Log:**

**Print:**

**Email/ Call:**

**Follow Up:**

**Pay/Submit:**

**Don't Forget:**

**Workflow Objective:**

**Phase 1: Initiate:**

**Phase 2: Execute:**

**Phase 3: Monitor:**

**Phase 4: Approve:**

**Phase 5: Wrap Up:**

**Critical Details:**

**Stakeholders:**

**Important Milestones:**

**Quick Contacts:**

| No. | Task: | Purpose: | Completion Date: | Completed? Yes No |
|-----|-------|----------|------------------|-------------------|
| 1   |       |          |                  |                   |
| 2   |       |          |                  |                   |
| 3   |       |          |                  |                   |
| 4   |       |          |                  |                   |
| 5   |       |          |                  |                   |
| 6   |       |          |                  |                   |
| 7   |       |          |                  |                   |
| 8   |       |          |                  |                   |
| 9   |       |          |                  |                   |
| 10  |       |          |                  |                   |
| 11  |       |          |                  |                   |
| 12  |       |          |                  |                   |
| 13  |       |          |                  |                   |
| 14  |       |          |                  |                   |
| 15  |       |          |                  |                   |
| 16  |       |          |                  |                   |
| 17  |       |          |                  |                   |
| 18  |       |          |                  |                   |
| 19  |       |          |                  |                   |
| 20  |       |          |                  |                   |
| 21  |       |          |                  |                   |
| 22  |       |          |                  |                   |
| 23  |       |          |                  |                   |
| 24  |       |          |                  |                   |

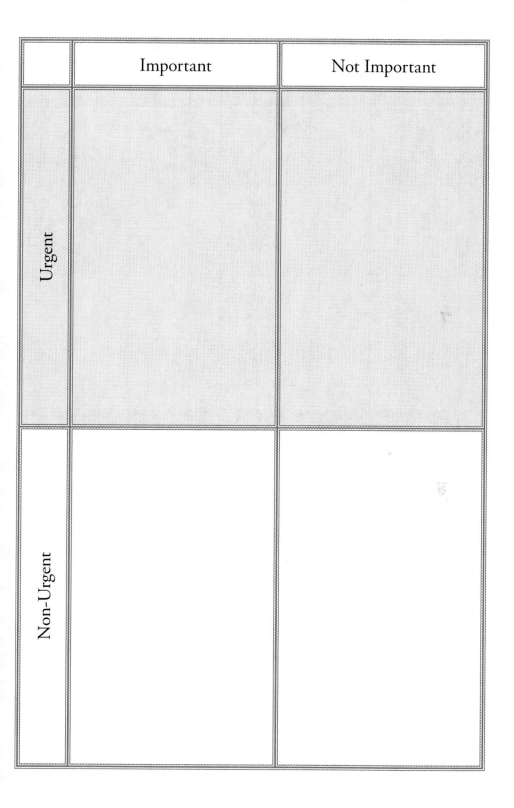

|  | Important | Not Important |
|---|---|---|
| Urgent | | |
| Non-Urgent | | |

| Important Dates: | Events/ Occasions: | Dress Attire: | Time: |
| --- | --- | --- | --- |
| | | | |
| | | | |
| | | | |
| | | | |
| | | | |
| | | | |
| | | | |
| | | | |
| | | | |
| | | | |
| | | | |
| | | | |

## Goals:
1.
2.
3.

## Tomorrow's Focus:
1.
2.
3.

## Work Motivation:
1.
2.
3.

## Personal Motivation:
1.
2.
3.

*Lingering Thoughts:*

**Project 24:**

**Month:**_____ **Week Of:**_____ **Start Date:**_____ **Due Date:**_____

**Priority:**

**Schedule/ Reschedule:**

**Inquire/ Look Into:**

**Log:**

**Print:**

**Email/ Call:**

**Follow Up:**

**Pay/Submit:**

**Don't Forget:**

**Workflow Objective:**

**Phase 1: Initiate:**

**Phase 2: Execute:**

**Phase 3: Monitor:**

**Phase 4: Approve:**

**Phase 5: Wrap Up:**

**Critical Details:**

**Stakeholders:**

**Important Milestones:**

**Quick Contacts:**

| No. | Task: | Purpose: | Completion Date: | Completed? Yes No |
|---|---|---|---|---|
| 1 | | | | |
| 2 | | | | |
| 3 | | | | |
| 4 | | | | |
| 5 | | | | |
| 6 | | | | |
| 7 | | | | |
| 8 | | | | |
| 9 | | | | |
| 10 | | | | |
| 11 | | | | |
| 12 | | | | |
| 13 | | | | |
| 14 | | | | |
| 15 | | | | |
| 16 | | | | |
| 17 | | | | |
| 18 | | | | |
| 19 | | | | |
| 20 | | | | |
| 21 | | | | |
| 22 | | | | |
| 23 | | | | |
| 24 | | | | |

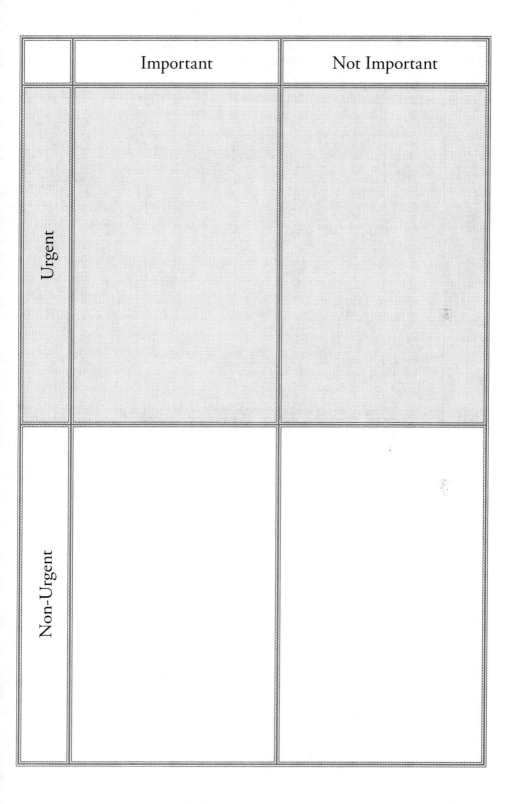

|  | Important | Not Important |
|---|---|---|
| **Urgent** | | |
| **Non-Urgent** | | |

| Important Dates: | Events/ Occasions: | Dress Attire: | Time: |
|---|---|---|---|
| | | | |
| | | | |
| | | | |
| | | | |
| | | | |
| | | | |
| | | | |
| | | | |
| | | | |
| | | | |
| | | | |
| | | | |
| | | | |

**Goals:**

1.

2.

3.


**Tomorrow's Focus:**

1.

2.

3.

**Work Motivation:**

1.

2.

3.

**Personal Motivation:**

1.

2.

3.

*Lingering Thoughts:*

**Project 25:**

**Month:**_____ **Week Of:**_____ **Start Date:**_____ **Due Date:**_____

**Priority:**

**Schedule/ Reschedule:**

**Inquire/ Look Into:**

**Log:**

**Print:**

**Email/ Call:**

**Follow Up:**

**Pay/Submit:**

**Don't Forget:**

**Workflow Objective:**

**Phase 1: Initiate:**

**Phase 2: Execute:**

**Phase 3: Monitor:**

**Phase 4: Approve:**

**Phase 5: Wrap Up:**

**Critical Details:**

**Stakeholders:**

**Important Milestones:**

**Quick Contacts:**

| No. | Task: | Purpose: | Completion Date: | Completed? Yes No | |
|---|---|---|---|---|---|
| 1 | | | | | |
| 2 | | | | | |
| 3 | | | | | |
| 4 | | | | | |
| 5 | | | | | |
| 6 | | | | | |
| 7 | | | | | |
| 8 | | | | | |
| 9 | | | | | |
| 10 | | | | | |
| 11 | | | | | |
| 12 | | | | | |
| 13 | | | | | |
| 14 | | | | | |
| 15 | | | | | |
| 16 | | | | | |
| 17 | | | | | |
| 18 | | | | | |
| 19 | | | | | |
| 20 | | | | | |
| 21 | | | | | |
| 22 | | | | | |
| 23 | | | | | |
| 24 | | | | | |

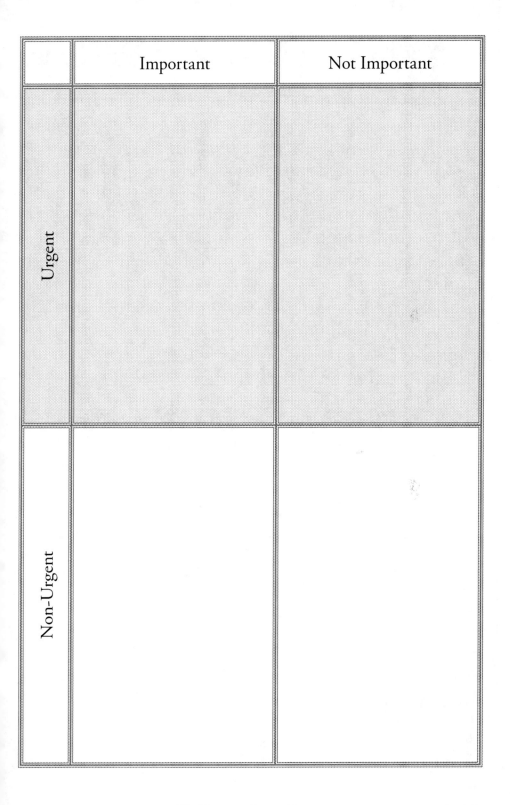

|  | Important | Not Important |
|---|---|---|
| Urgent |  |  |
| Non-Urgent |  |  |

| Important Dates: | Events/ Occasions: | Dress Attire: | Time: |
|---|---|---|---|
| | | | |
| | | | |
| | | | |
| | | | |
| | | | |
| | | | |
| | | | |
| | | | |
| | | | |
| | | | |
| | | | |
| | | | |
| | | | |

## Goals:
1.
2.
3.

## Tomorrow's Focus:
1.
2.
3.

## Work Motivation:
1.
2.
3.

## Personal Motivation:
1.
2.
3.

*The Blueprint: Project Planner*

*Lingering Thoughts:*

**Project 26:**

**Month:_____ Week Of:_____ Start Date:_____ Due Date:_____**

**Priority:**

**Schedule/ Reschedule:**

**Inquire/ Look Into:**

**Log:**

**Print:**

**Email/ Call:**

**Follow Up:**

**Pay/Submit:**

**Don't Forget:**

**Workflow Objective:**

**Phase 1: Initiate:**

**Phase 2: Execute:**

**Phase 3: Monitor:**

**Phase 4: Approve:**

**Phase 5: Wrap Up:**

**Critical Details:**

**Stakeholders:**

**Important Milestones:**

**Quick Contacts:**

| No. | Task: | Purpose: | Completion Date: | Completed? Yes No |
| --- | --- | --- | --- | --- |
| 1 | | | | |
| 2 | | | | |
| 3 | | | | |
| 4 | | | | |
| 5 | | | | |
| 6 | | | | |
| 7 | | | | |
| 8 | | | | |
| 9 | | | | |
| 10 | | | | |
| 11 | | | | |
| 12 | | | | |
| 13 | | | | |
| 14 | | | | |
| 15 | | | | |
| 16 | | | | |
| 17 | | | | |
| 18 | | | | |
| 19 | | | | |
| 20 | | | | |
| 21 | | | | |
| 22 | | | | |
| 23 | | | | |
| 24 | | | | |

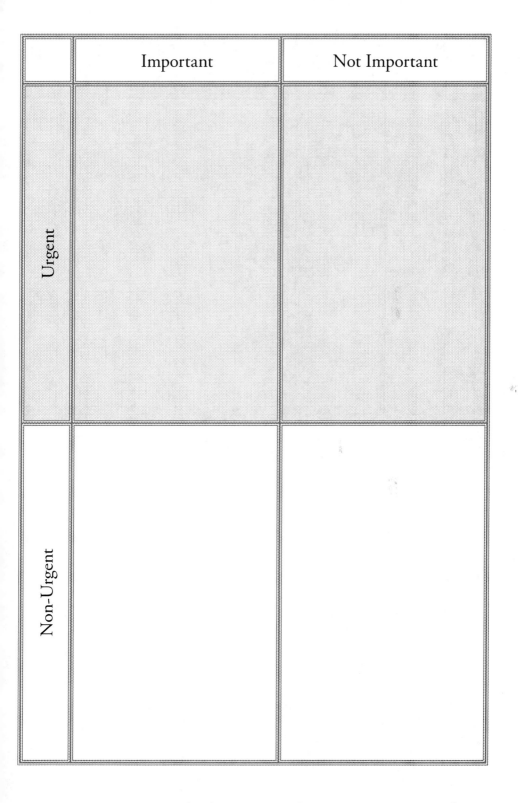

|  | Important | Not Important |
|---|---|---|
| **Urgent** | | |
| **Non-Urgent** | | |

| Important Dates: | Events/ Occasions: | Dress Attire: | Time: |
|---|---|---|---|
| | | | |
| | | | |
| | | | |
| | | | |
| | | | |
| | | | |
| | | | |
| | | | |
| | | | |
| | | | |
| | | | |

## Goals:
1.
2.
3.

## Tomorrow's Focus:
1.
2.
3.

## Work Motivation:
1.
2.
3.

## Personal Motivation:
1.
2.
3.

*Lingering Thoughts:*

**Project 27:**

**Month:_____ Week Of:_____ Start Date:_____ Due Date:_____**

**Priority:**

**Schedule/ Reschedule:**

**Inquire/ Look Into:**

**Log:**

**Print:**

**Email/ Call:**

**Follow Up:**

**Pay/Submit:**

**Don't Forget:**

**Workflow Objective:**

**Phase 1: Initiate:**

**Phase 2: Execute:**

**Phase 3: Monitor:**

**Phase 4: Approve:**

**Phase 5: Wrap Up:**

**Critical Details:**

**Stakeholders:**

**Important Milestones:**

**Quick Contacts:**

| No. | Task: | Purpose: | Completion Date: | Completed? Yes No | |
|-----|-------|----------|------------------|------|------|
| 1 | | | | | |
| 2 | | | | | |
| 3 | | | | | |
| 4 | | | | | |
| 5 | | | | | |
| 6 | | | | | |
| 7 | | | | | |
| 8 | | | | | |
| 9 | | | | | |
| 10 | | | | | |
| 11 | | | | | |
| 12 | | | | | |
| 13 | | | | | |
| 14 | | | | | |
| 15 | | | | | |
| 16 | | | | | |
| 17 | | | | | |
| 18 | | | | | |
| 19 | | | | | |
| 20 | | | | | |
| 21 | | | | | |
| 22 | | | | | |
| 23 | | | | | |
| 24 | | | | | |

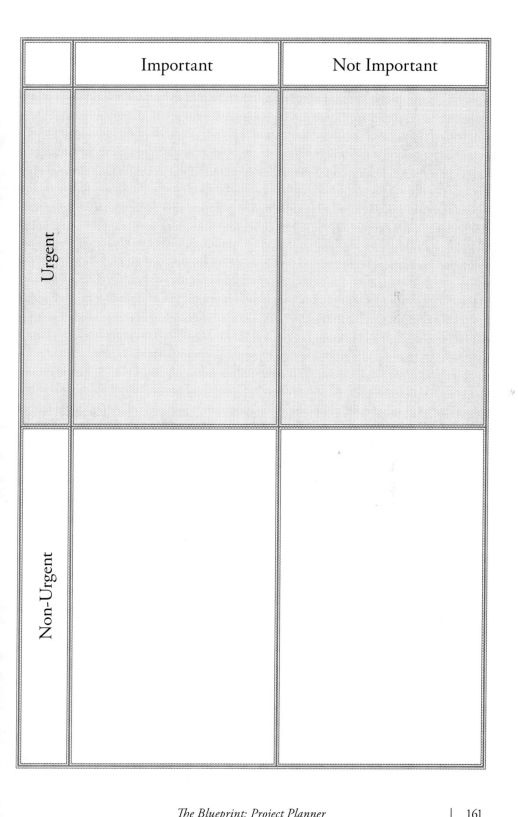

| | Important | Not Important |
|---|---|---|
| **Urgent** | | |
| **Non-Urgent** | | |

| Important Dates: | Events/ Occasions: | Dress Attire: | Time: |
|---|---|---|---|
| | | | |
| | | | |
| | | | |
| | | | |
| | | | |
| | | | |
| | | | |
| | | | |
| | | | |
| | | | |
| | | | |
| | | | |
| | | | |

## Goals:
1.
2.
3.

## Tomorrow's Focus:
1.
2.
3.

## Work Motivation:
1.
2.
3.

## Personal Motivation:
1.
2.
3.

*The Blueprint: Project Planner*

*Lingering Thoughts:*

**Project 28:**

**Month:**_____ **Week Of:**_____ **Start Date:**_____ **Due Date:**_____

**Priority:**

**Schedule/ Reschedule:**

**Inquire/ Look Into:**

**Log:**

**Print:**

**Email/ Call:**

**Follow Up:**

**Pay/Submit:**

**Don't Forget:**

**Workflow Objective:**

**Phase 1: Initiate:**

**Phase 2: Execute:**

**Phase 3: Monitor:**

**Phase 4: Approve:**

**Phase 5: Wrap Up:**

**Critical Details:**

**Stakeholders:**

**Important Milestones:**

**Quick Contacts:**

| No. | Task: | Purpose: | Completion Date: | Completed? Yes No | |
|-----|-------|----------|------------------|-----|-----|
| 1 | | | | | |
| 2 | | | | | |
| 3 | | | | | |
| 4 | | | | | |
| 5 | | | | | |
| 6 | | | | | |
| 7 | | | | | |
| 8 | | | | | |
| 9 | | | | | |
| 10 | | | | | |
| 11 | | | | | |
| 12 | | | | | |
| 13 | | | | | |
| 14 | | | | | |
| 15 | | | | | |
| 16 | | | | | |
| 17 | | | | | |
| 18 | | | | | |
| 19 | | | | | |
| 20 | | | | | |
| 21 | | | | | |
| 22 | | | | | |
| 23 | | | | | |
| 24 | | | | | |

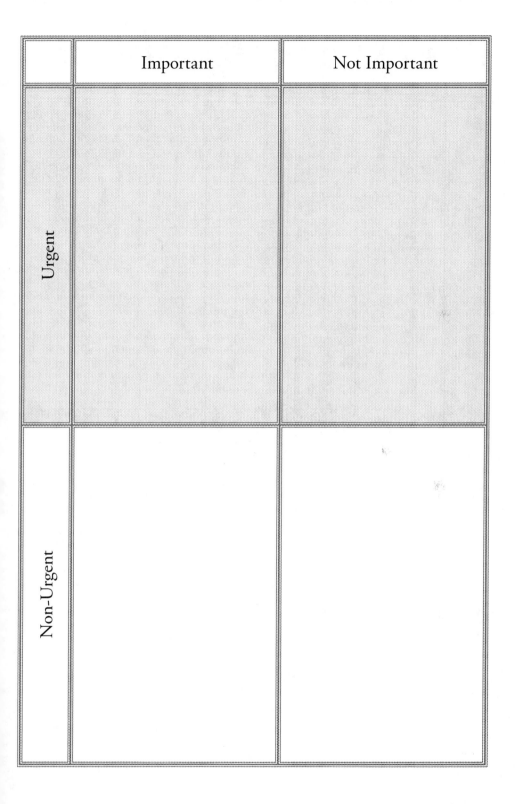

|  | Important | Not Important |
|---|---|---|
| **Urgent** | | |
| **Non-Urgent** | | |

| Important Dates: | Events/ Occasions: | Dress Attire: | Time: |
|---|---|---|---|
| | | | |
| | | | |
| | | | |
| | | | |
| | | | |
| | | | |
| | | | |
| | | | |
| | | | |
| | | | |
| | | | |
| | | | |

**Goals:**

1.

2.

3.

**Tomorrow's Focus:**

1.

2.

3.

**Work Motivation:**

1.

2.

3.

**Personal Motivation:**

1.

2.

3.

*The Blueprint: Project Planner*

*Lingering Thoughts:*

**Project 29:**

Month:_____ Week Of:_____ Start Date:_____ Due Date:_____

**Priority:**

**Schedule/ Reschedule:**

**Inquire/ Look Into:**

**Log:**

**Print:**

**Email/ Call:**

**Follow Up:**

**Pay/Submit:**

**Don't Forget:**

**Workflow Objective:**

**Phase 1: Initiate:**

**Phase 2: Execute:**

**Phase 3: Monitor:**

**Phase 4: Approve:**

**Phase 5: Wrap Up:**

**Critical Details:**

**Stakeholders:**

**Important Milestones:**

**Quick Contacts:**

| No. | Task: | Purpose: | Completion Date: | Completed? | |
|-----|-------|----------|------------------|------------|---|
| | | | | Yes | No |
| 1 | | | | | |
| 2 | | | | | |
| 3 | | | | | |
| 4 | | | | | |
| 5 | | | | | |
| 6 | | | | | |
| 7 | | | | | |
| 8 | | | | | |
| 9 | | | | | |
| 10 | | | | | |
| 11 | | | | | |
| 12 | | | | | |
| 13 | | | | | |
| 14 | | | | | |
| 15 | | | | | |
| 16 | | | | | |
| 17 | | | | | |
| 18 | | | | | |
| 19 | | | | | |
| 20 | | | | | |
| 21 | | | | | |
| 22 | | | | | |
| 23 | | | | | |
| 24 | | | | | |

| | Important | Not Important |
|---|---|---|
| **Urgent** | | |
| **Non-Urgent** | | |

| Important Dates: | Events/ Occasions: | Dress Attire: | Time: |
|---|---|---|---|
| | | | |
| | | | |
| | | | |
| | | | |
| | | | |
| | | | |
| | | | |
| | | | |
| | | | |
| | | | |
| | | | |
| | | | |
| | | | |

**Goals:**

1.
2.
3.

**Tomorrow's Focus:**

1.
2.
3.

**Work Motivation:**

1.
2.
3.

**Personal Motivation:**

1.
2.
3.

*Lingering Thoughts:*

**Project 30:**

Month:_____ Week Of:_____ Start Date:_____ Due Date:_____

**Priority:**

**Schedule/ Reschedule:**

**Inquire/ Look Into:**

**Log:**

**Print:**

**Email/ Call:**

**Follow Up:**

**Pay/Submit:**

**Don't Forget:**

**Workflow Objective:**

**Phase 1: Initiate:**

**Phase 2: Execute:**

**Phase 3: Monitor:**

**Phase 4: Approve:**

**Phase 5: Wrap Up:**

**Critical Details:**

**Stakeholders:**

**Important Milestones:**

**Quick Contacts:**

| No. | Task: | Purpose: | Completion Date: | Completed? Yes No |
|---|---|---|---|---|
| 1 | | | | |
| 2 | | | | |
| 3 | | | | |
| 4 | | | | |
| 5 | | | | |
| 6 | | | | |
| 7 | | | | |
| 8 | | | | |
| 9 | | | | |
| 10 | | | | |
| 11 | | | | |
| 12 | | | | |
| 13 | | | | |
| 14 | | | | |
| 15 | | | | |
| 16 | | | | |
| 17 | | | | |
| 18 | | | | |
| 19 | | | | |
| 20 | | | | |
| 21 | | | | |
| 22 | | | | |
| 23 | | | | |
| 24 | | | | |

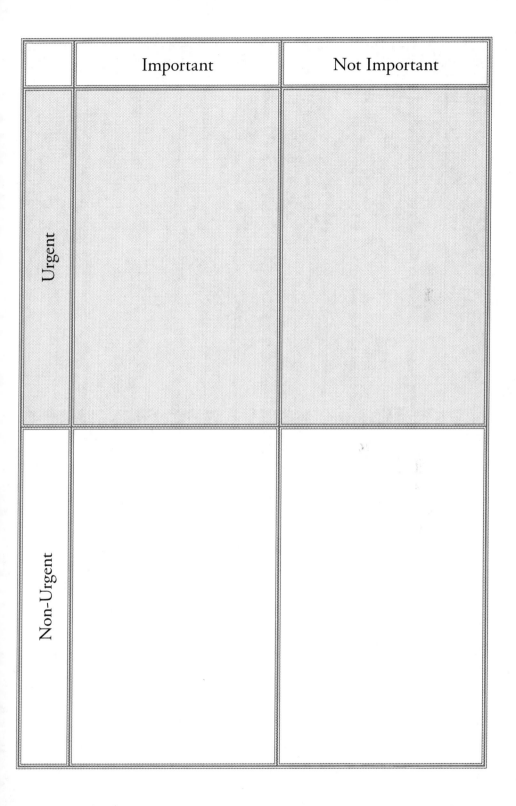

|  | Important | Not Important |
|---|---|---|
| **Urgent** | | |
| **Non-Urgent** | | |

| Important Dates: | Events/ Occasions: | Dress Attire: | Time: |
| --- | --- | --- | --- |
| | | | |
| | | | |
| | | | |
| | | | |
| | | | |
| | | | |
| | | | |
| | | | |
| | | | |
| | | | |
| | | | |

| Goals: |
| --- |
| 1. |
| 2. |
| 3. |
| |

| Tomorrow's Focus: |
| --- |
| 1. |
| 2. |
| 3. |
| |

| Work Motivation: |
| --- |
| 1. |
| 2. |
| 3. |
| |

| Personal Motivation: |
| --- |
| 1. |
| 2. |
| 3. |
| |

*Lingering Thoughts:*

**Reference Page**

Important Contacts:

| No. | Name: | Affiliation: | Contact #: | Email: |
|-----|-------|--------------|------------|--------|
| 1 | | | | |
| 2 | | | | |
| 3 | | | | |
| 4 | | | | |
| 5 | | | | |
| 6 | | | | |
| 7 | | | | |
| 8 | | | | |
| 9 | | | | |
| 10 | | | | |
| 11 | | | | |
| 12 | | | | |
| 13 | | | | |
| 14 | | | | |
| 15 | | | | |
| 16 | | | | |
| 17 | | | | |
| 18 | | | | |
| 19 | | | | |
| 20 | | | | |
| 21 | | | | |
| 22 | | | | |
| 23 | | | | |
| 24 | | | | |

| No. | Name: | Affiliation: | Contact #: | Email: |
|-----|-------|-------------|------------|--------|
| 25  |       |             |            |        |
| 26  |       |             |            |        |
| 27  |       |             |            |        |
| 28  |       |             |            |        |
| 29  |       |             |            |        |
| 30  |       |             |            |        |
| 31  |       |             |            |        |
| 32  |       |             |            |        |
| 33  |       |             |            |        |
| 34  |       |             |            |        |
| 35  |       |             |            |        |
| 36  |       |             |            |        |
| 37  |       |             |            |        |
| 38  |       |             |            |        |
| 39  |       |             |            |        |
| 40  |       |             |            |        |
| 41  |       |             |            |        |
| 42  |       |             |            |        |
| 43  |       |             |            |        |
| 44  |       |             |            |        |
| 45  |       |             |            |        |
| 46  |       |             |            |        |
| 47  |       |             |            |        |
| 48  |       |             |            |        |